FARM ANIMAL

COLORING BOOK

this book belongs to:

____

____

____

COLOR TEST

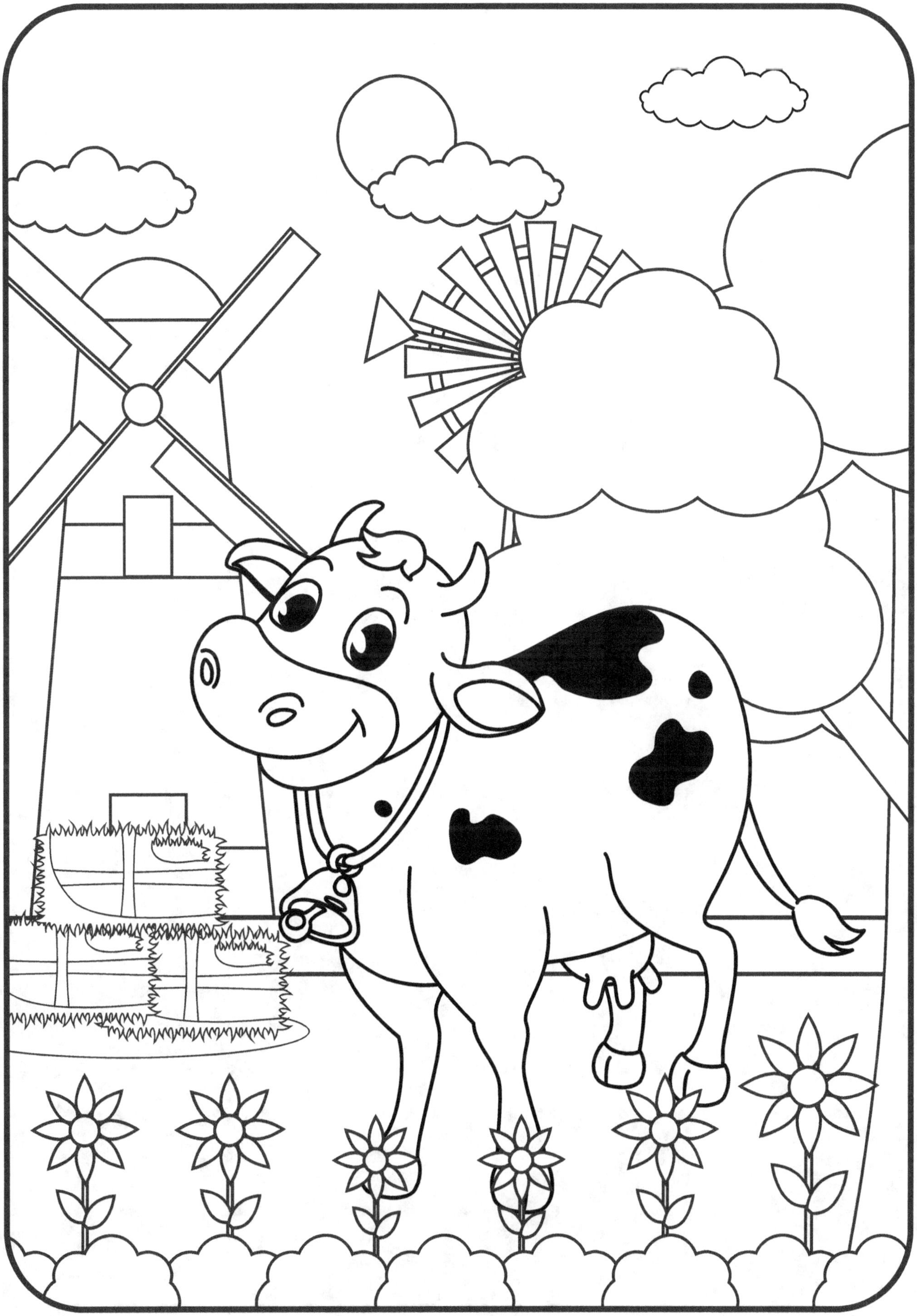

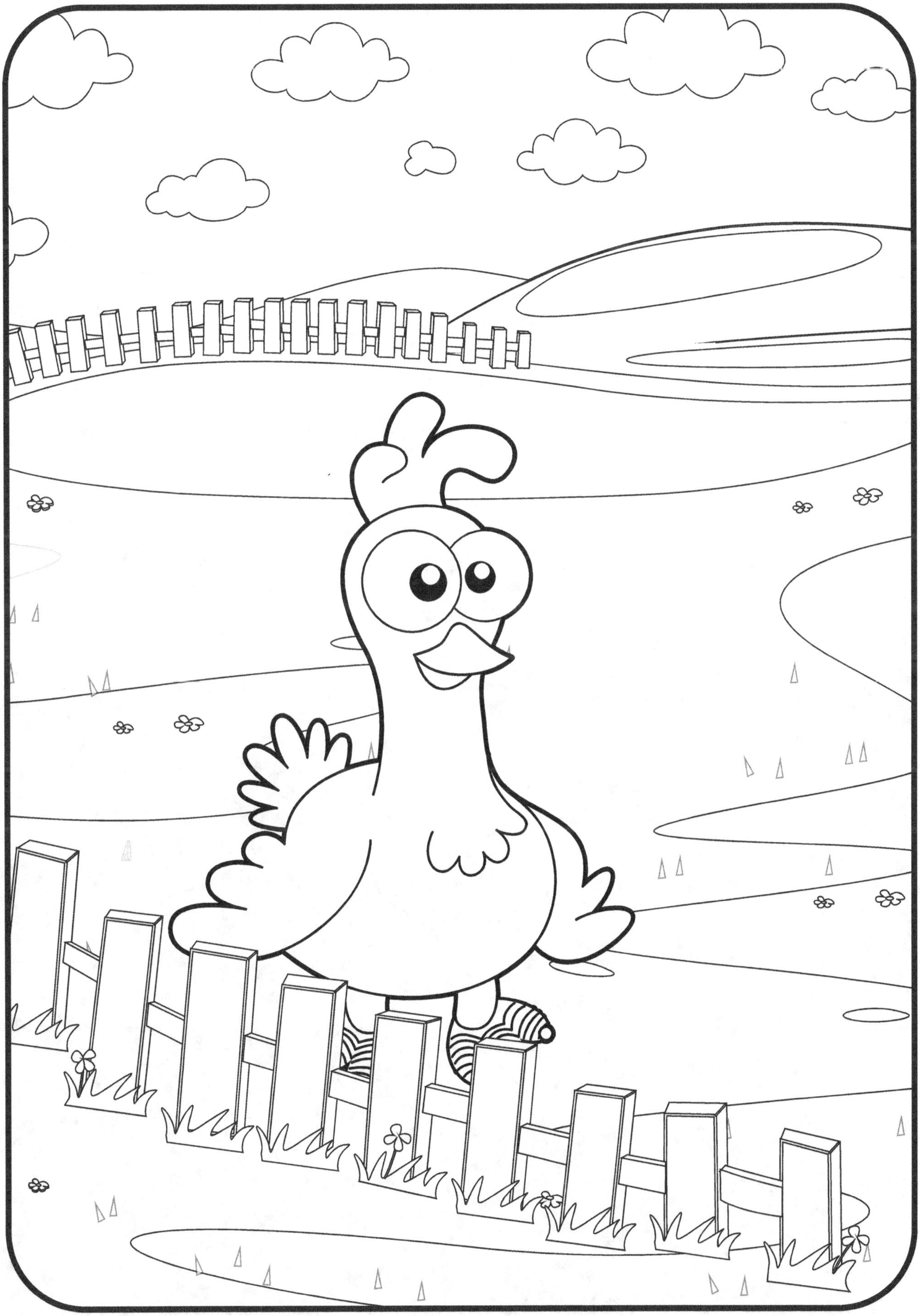

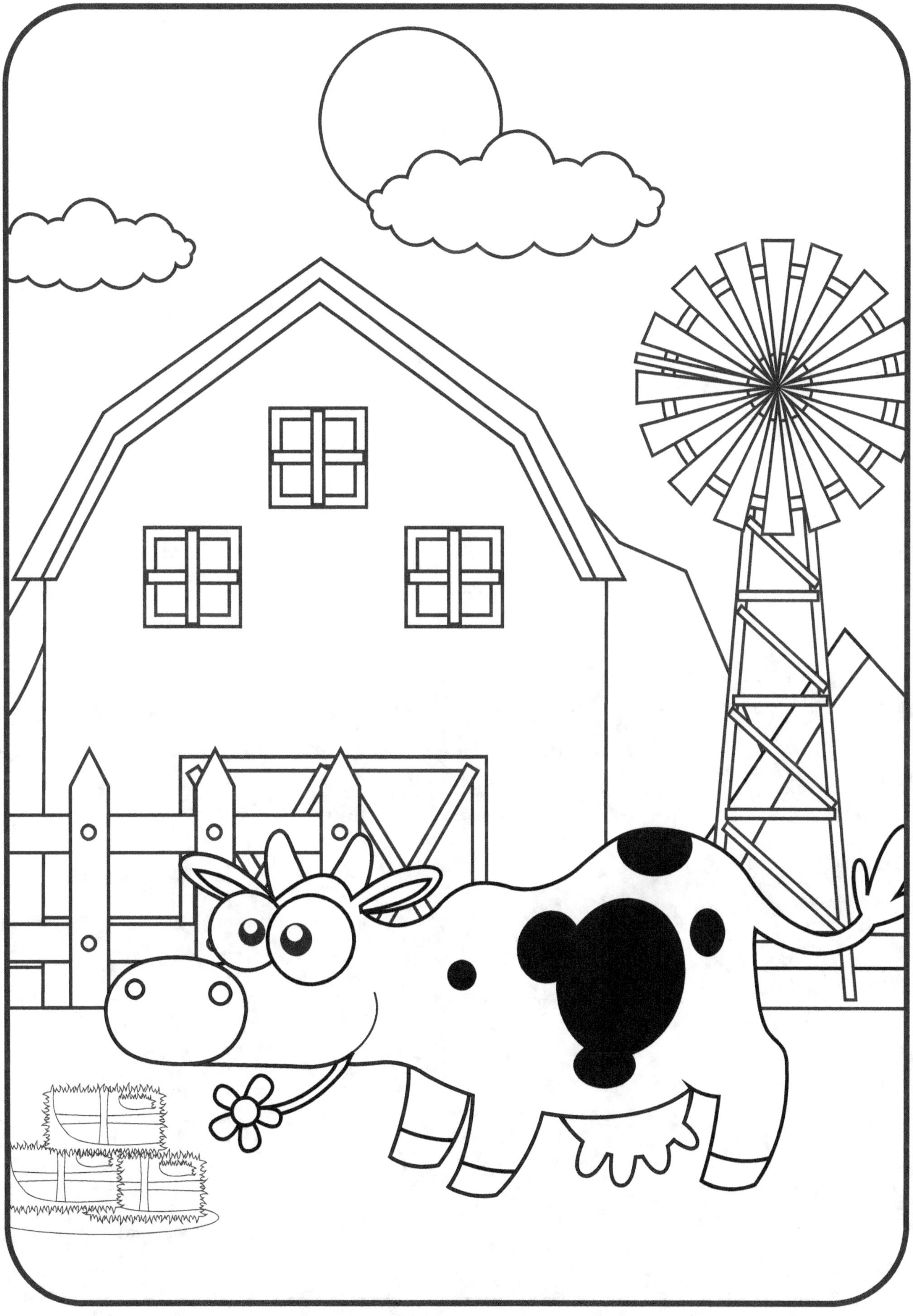

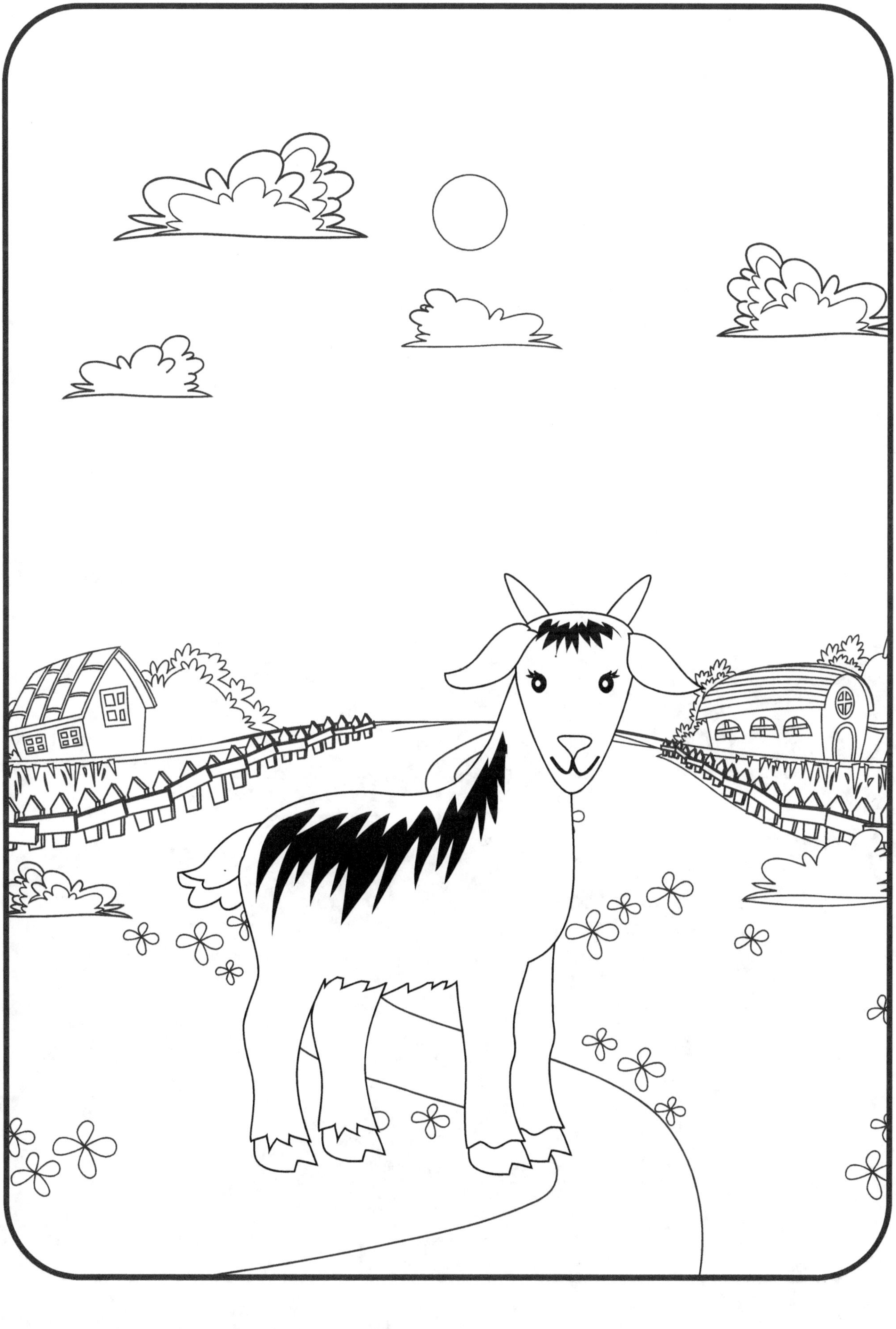

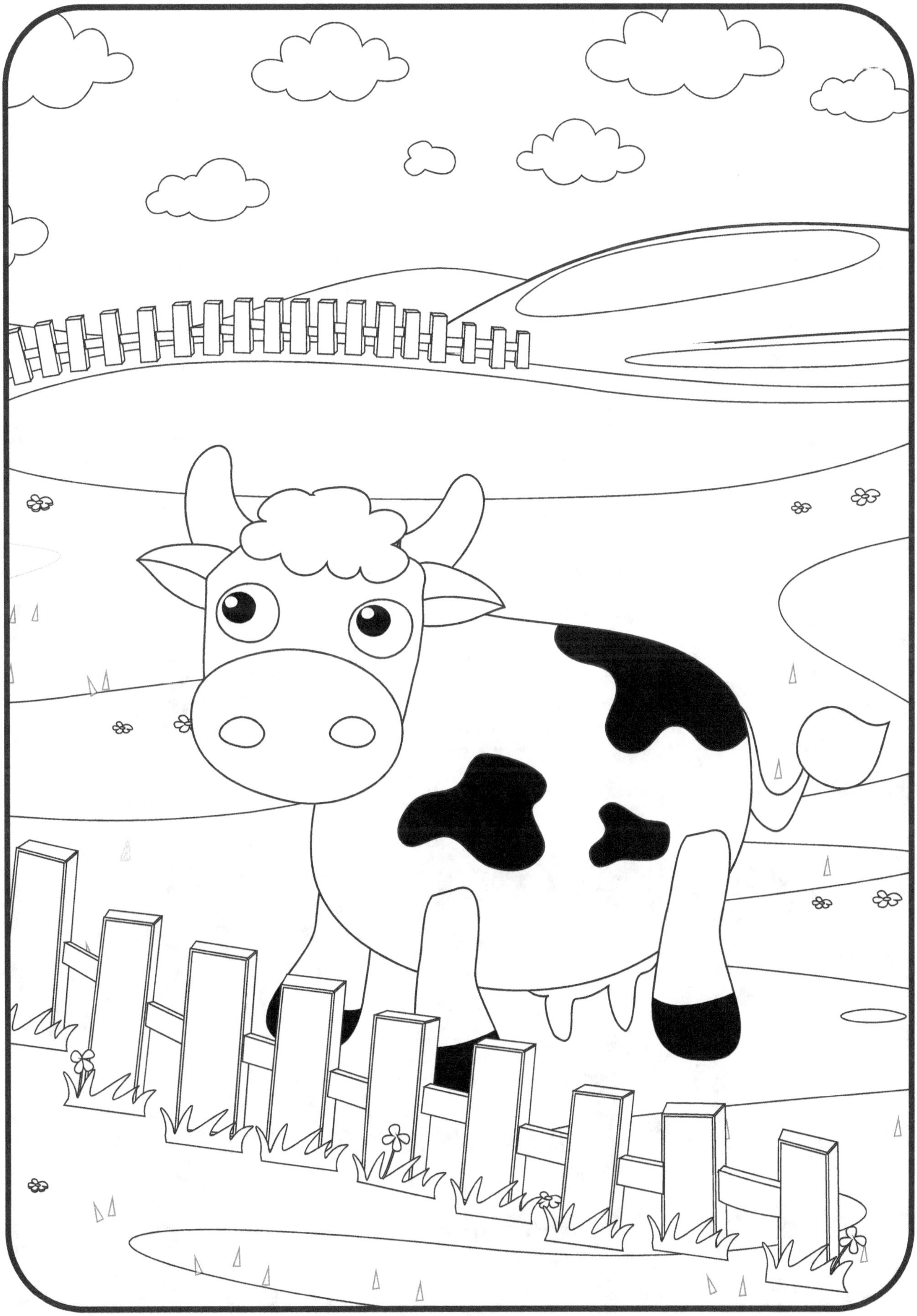

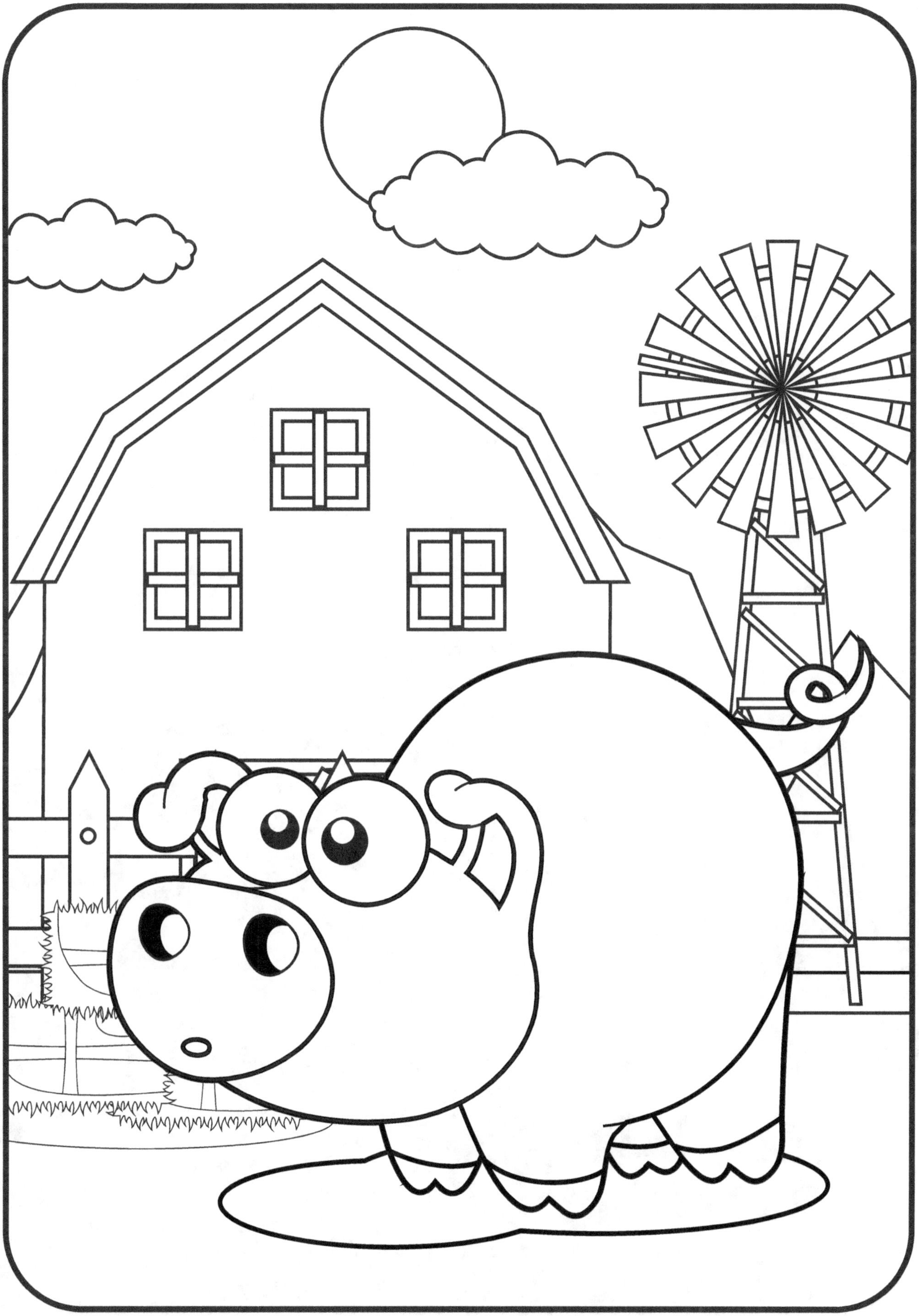

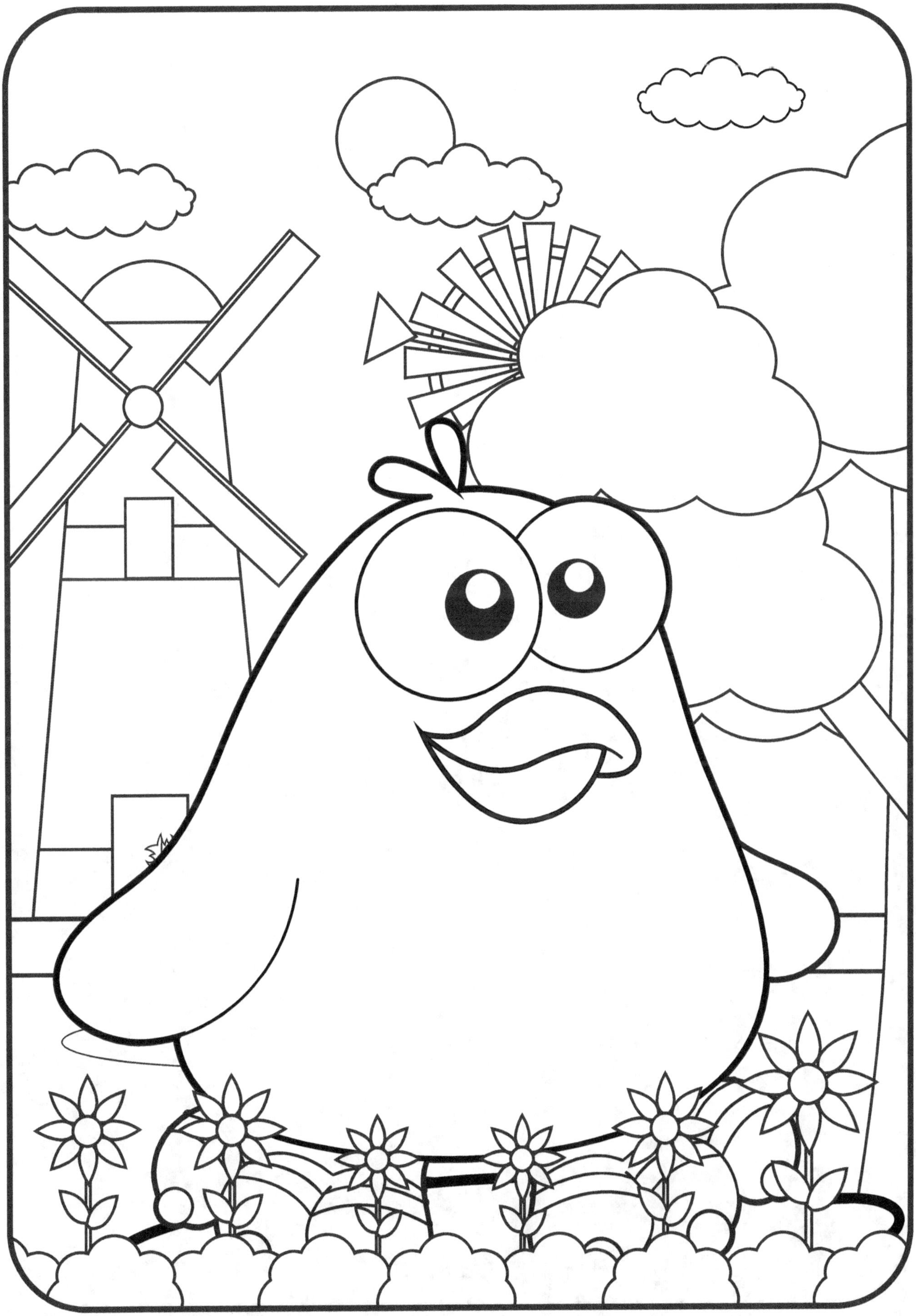

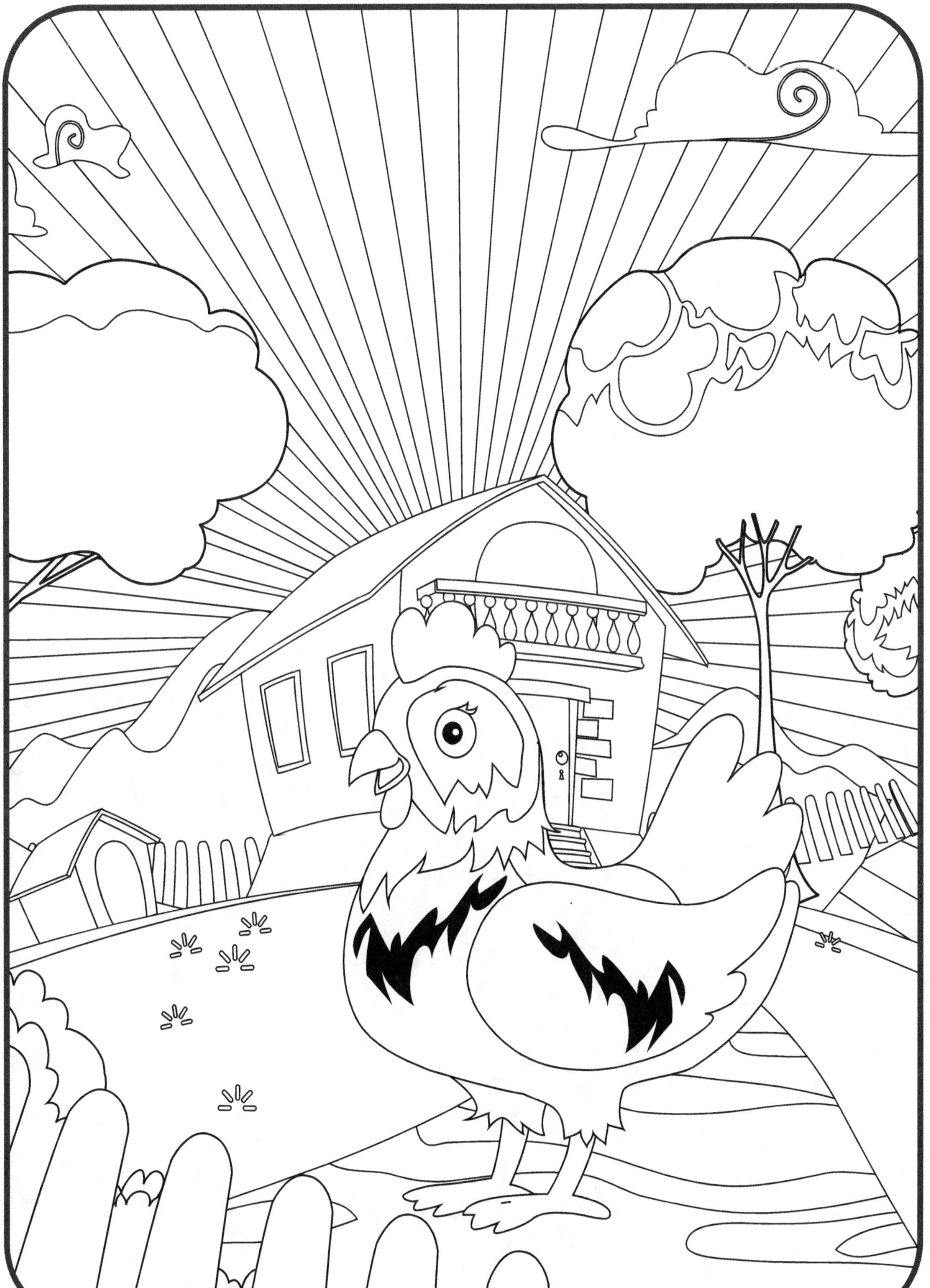

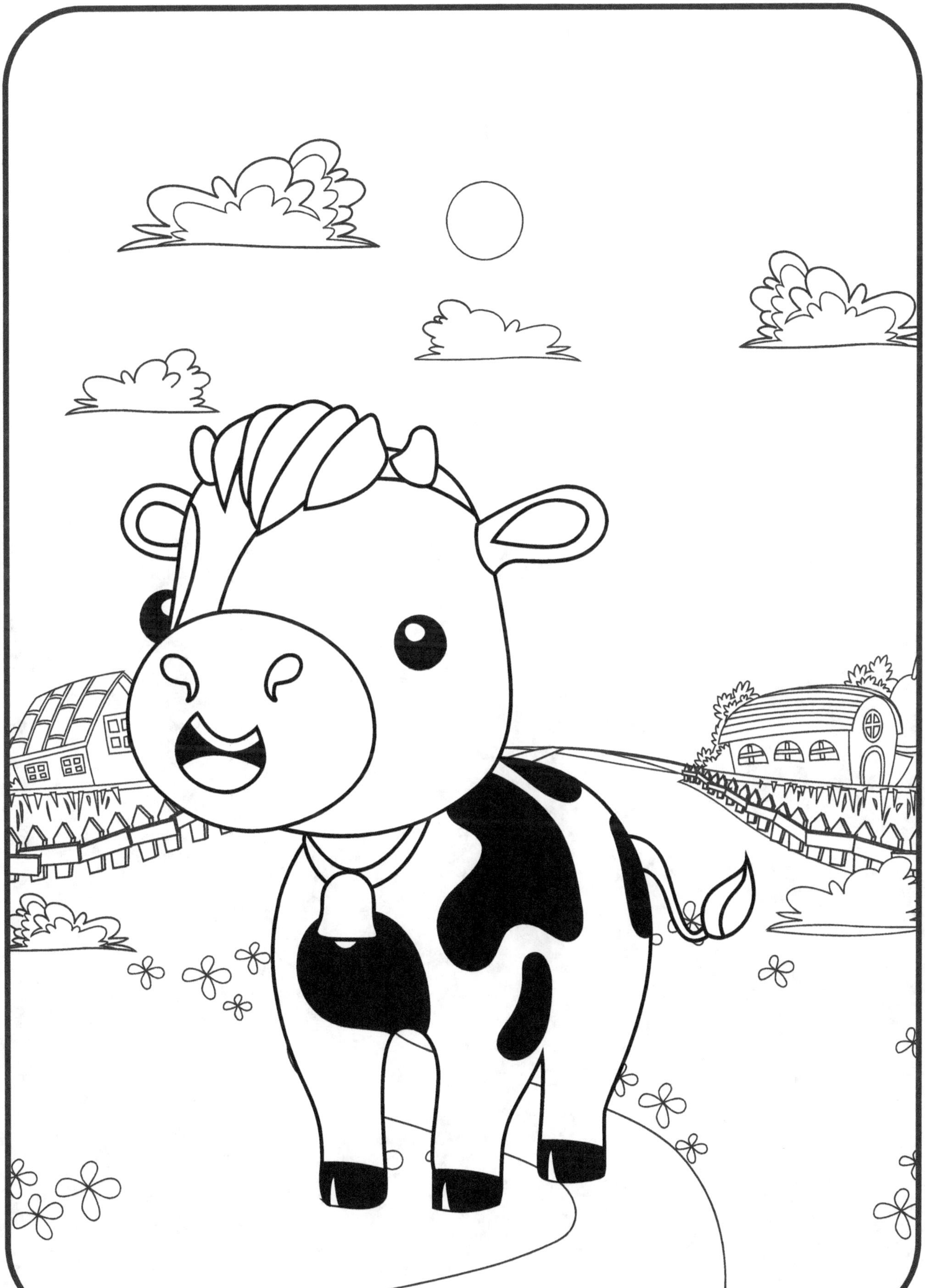

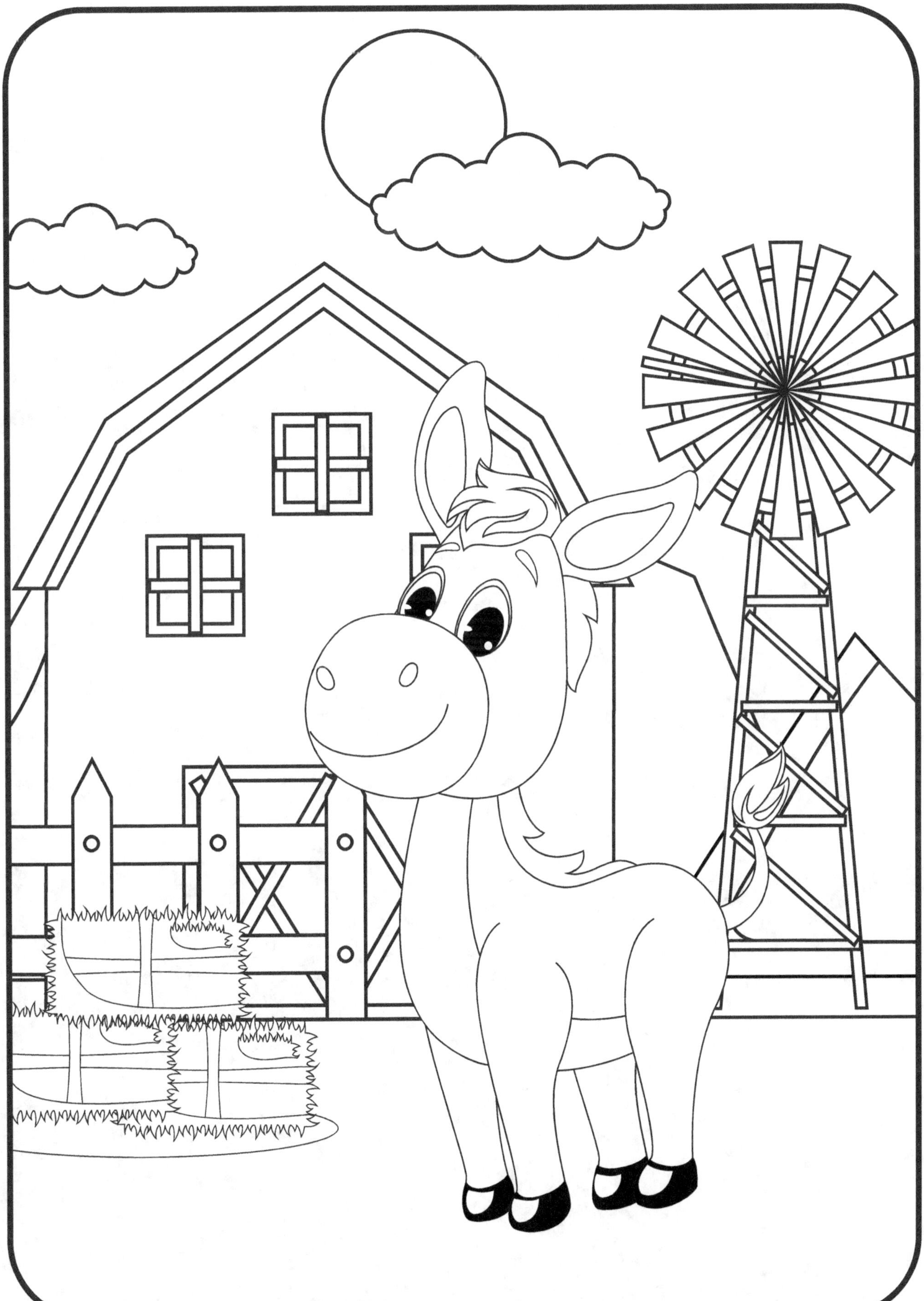

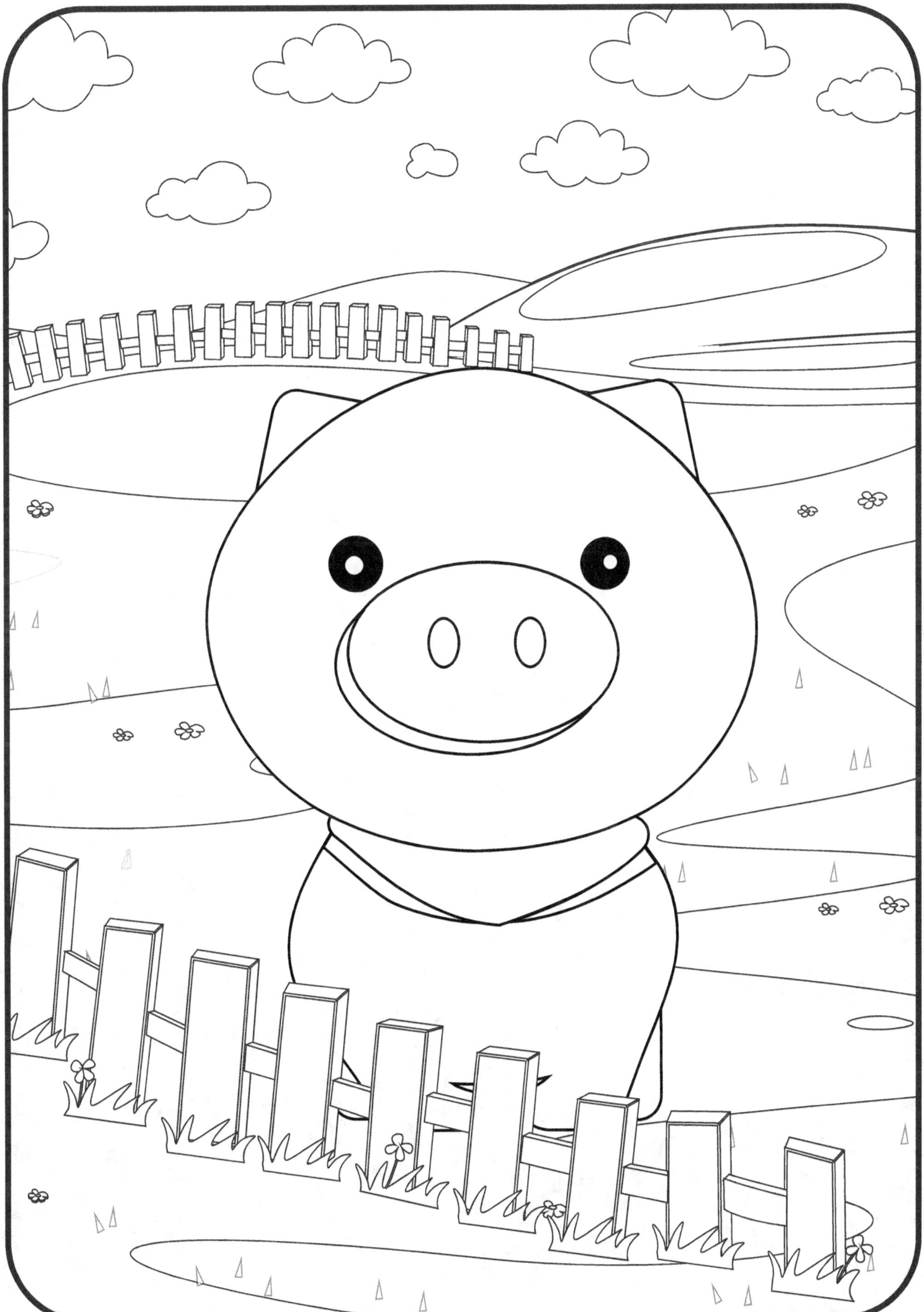

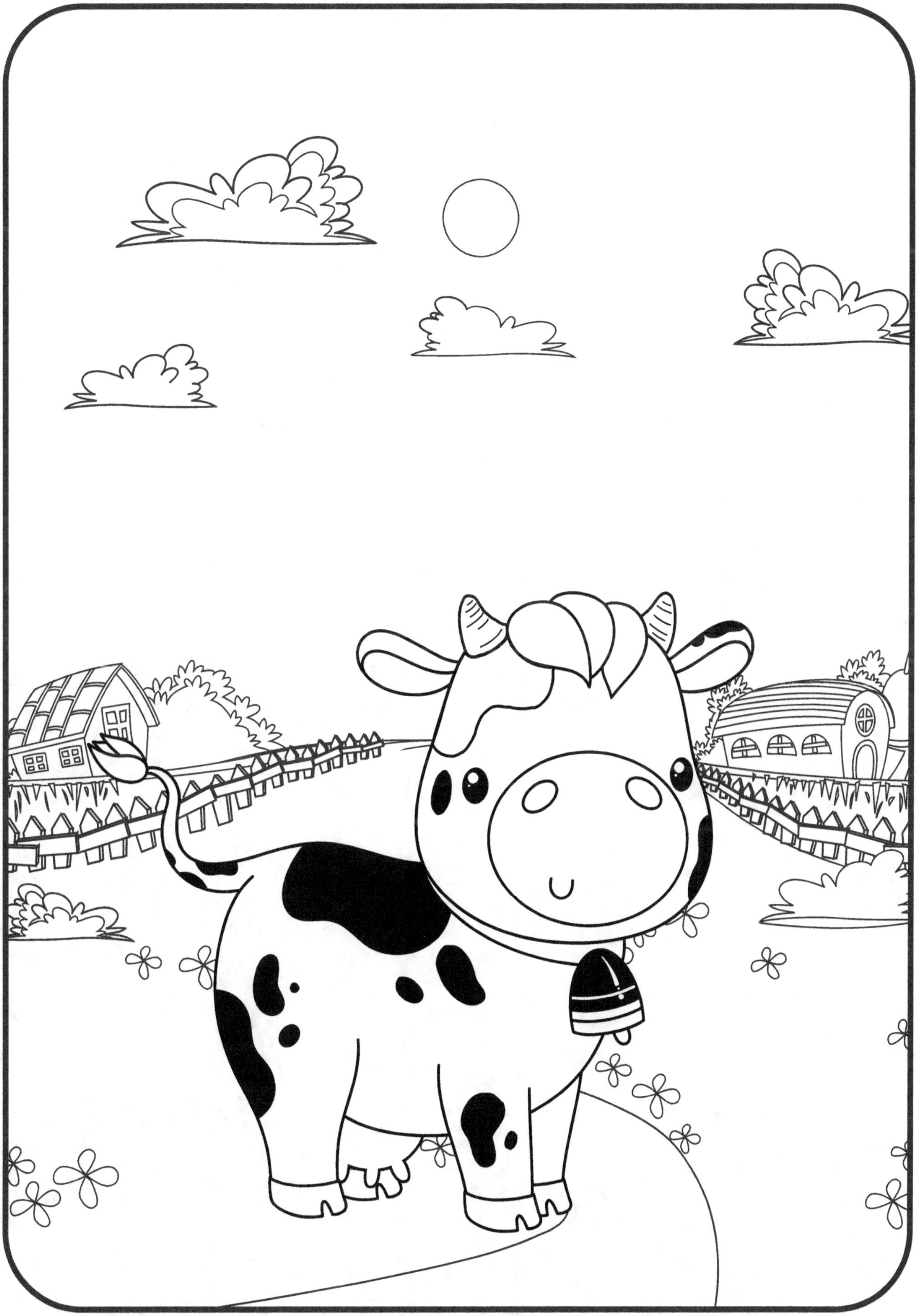

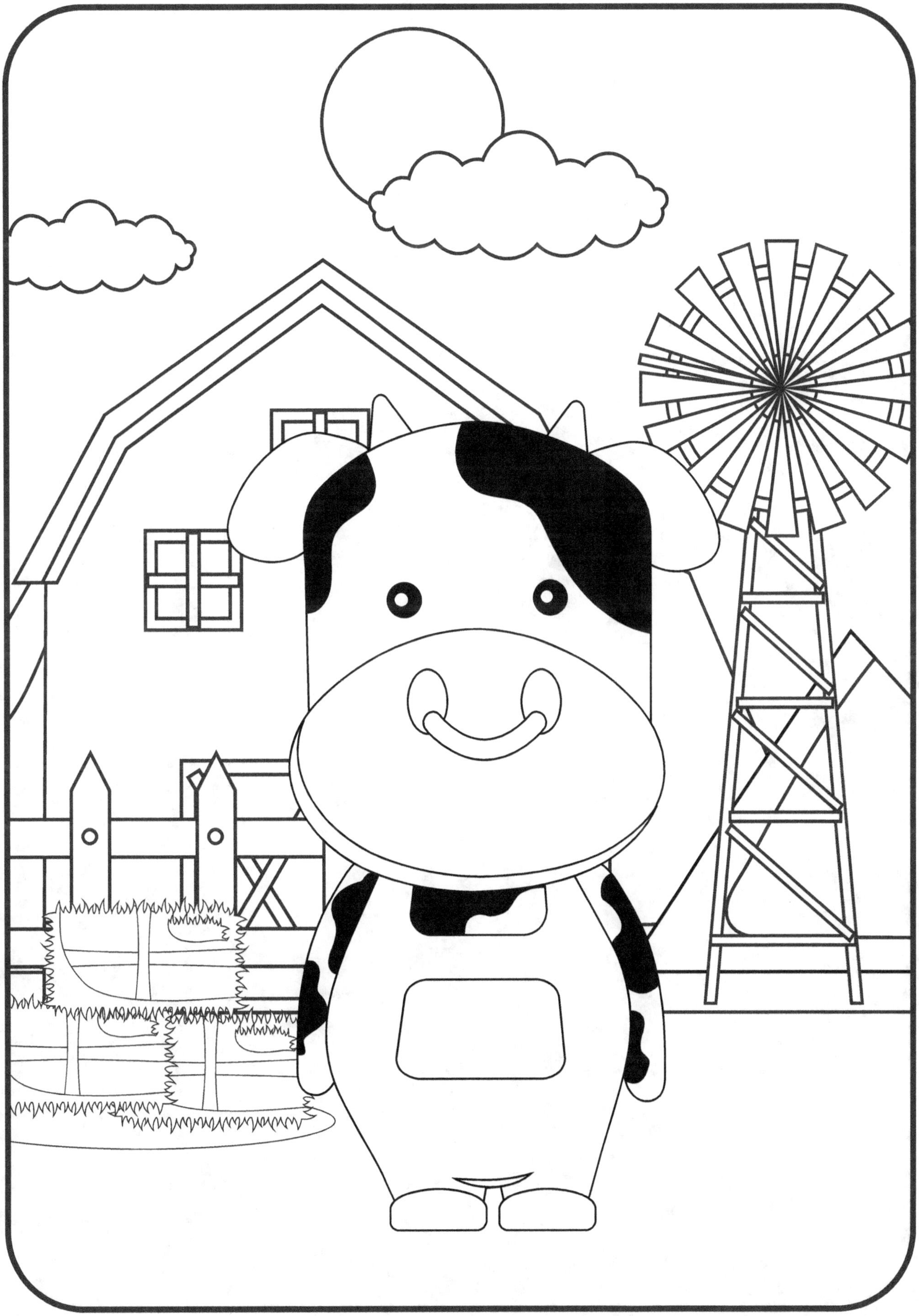

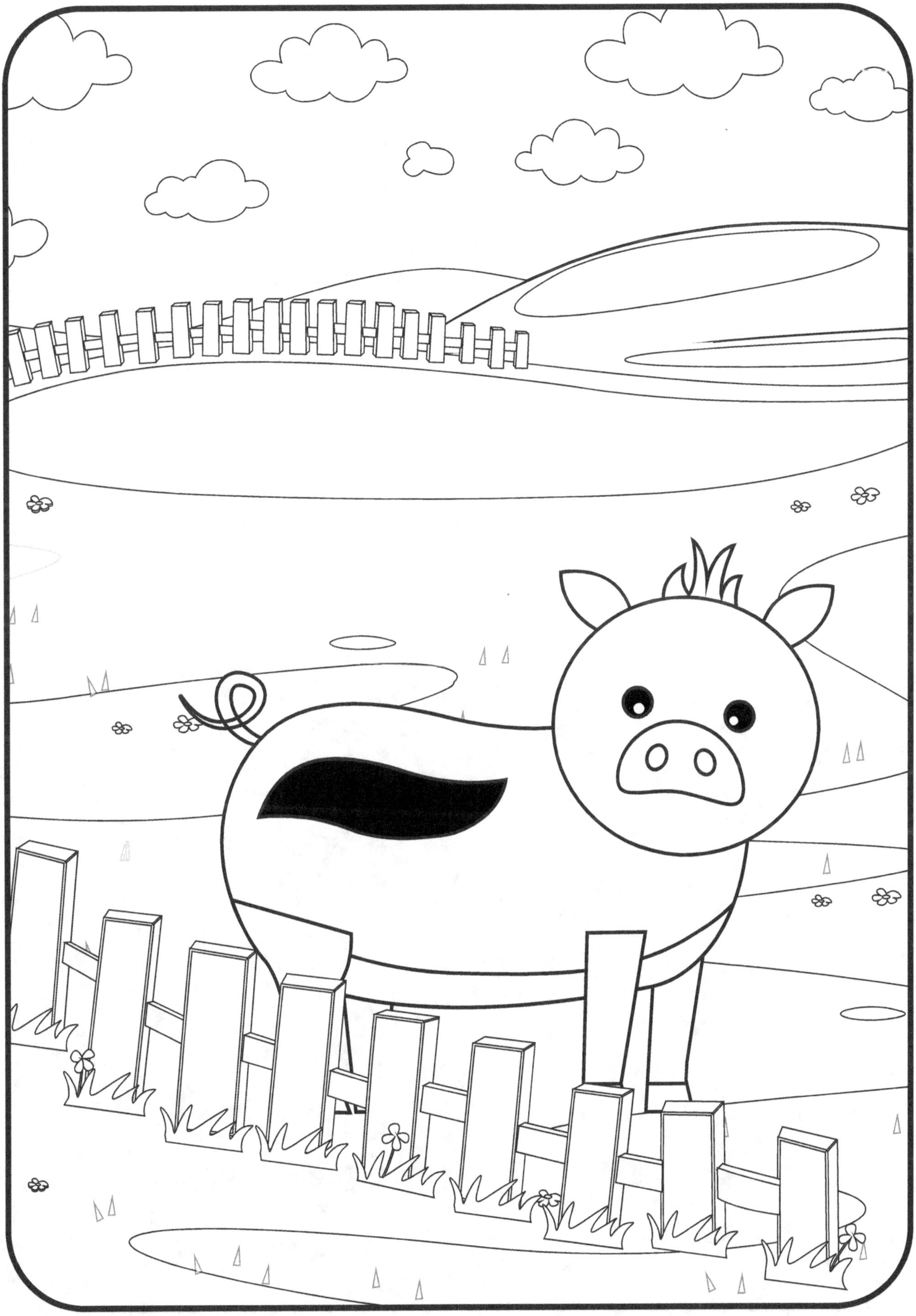

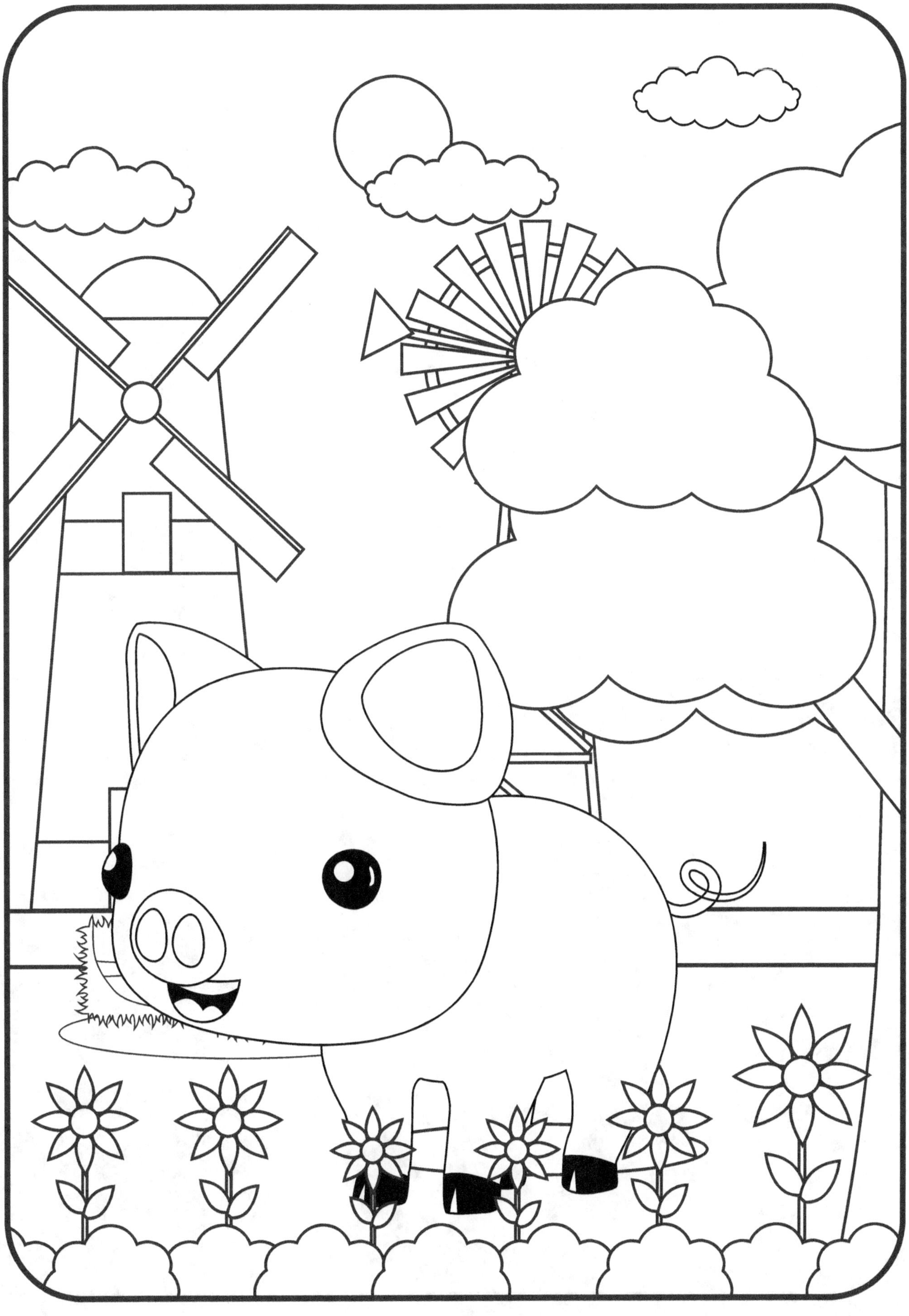

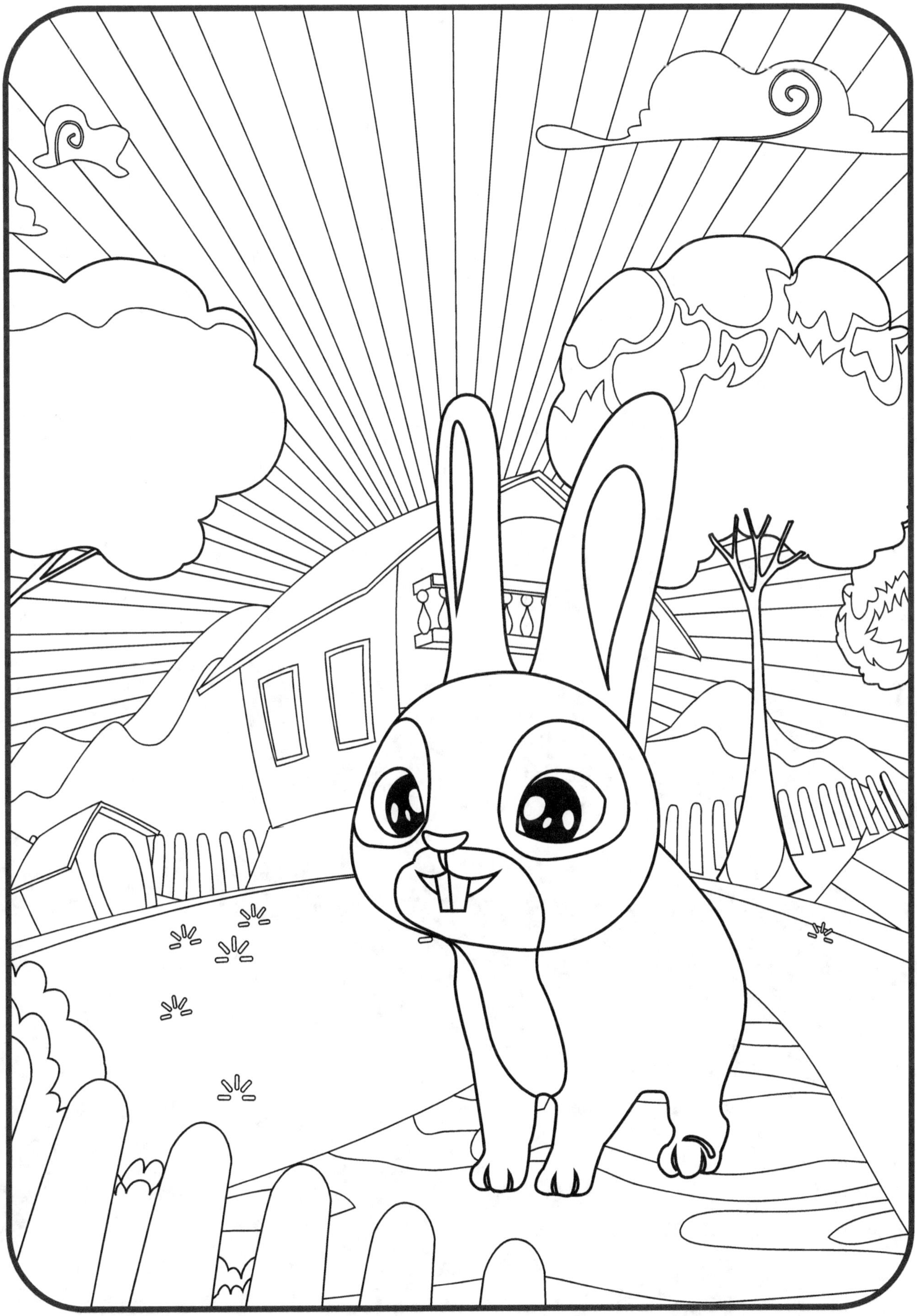

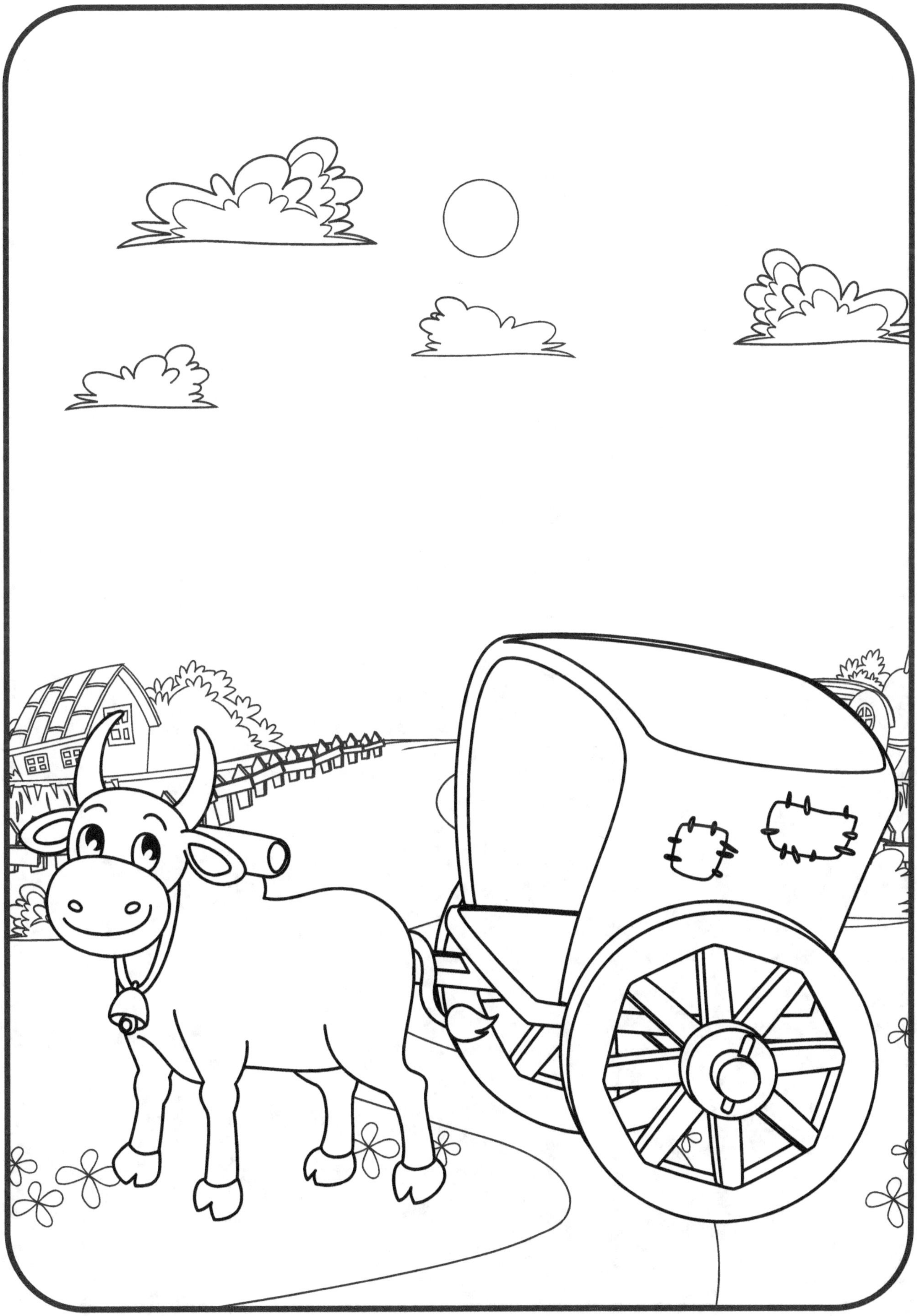

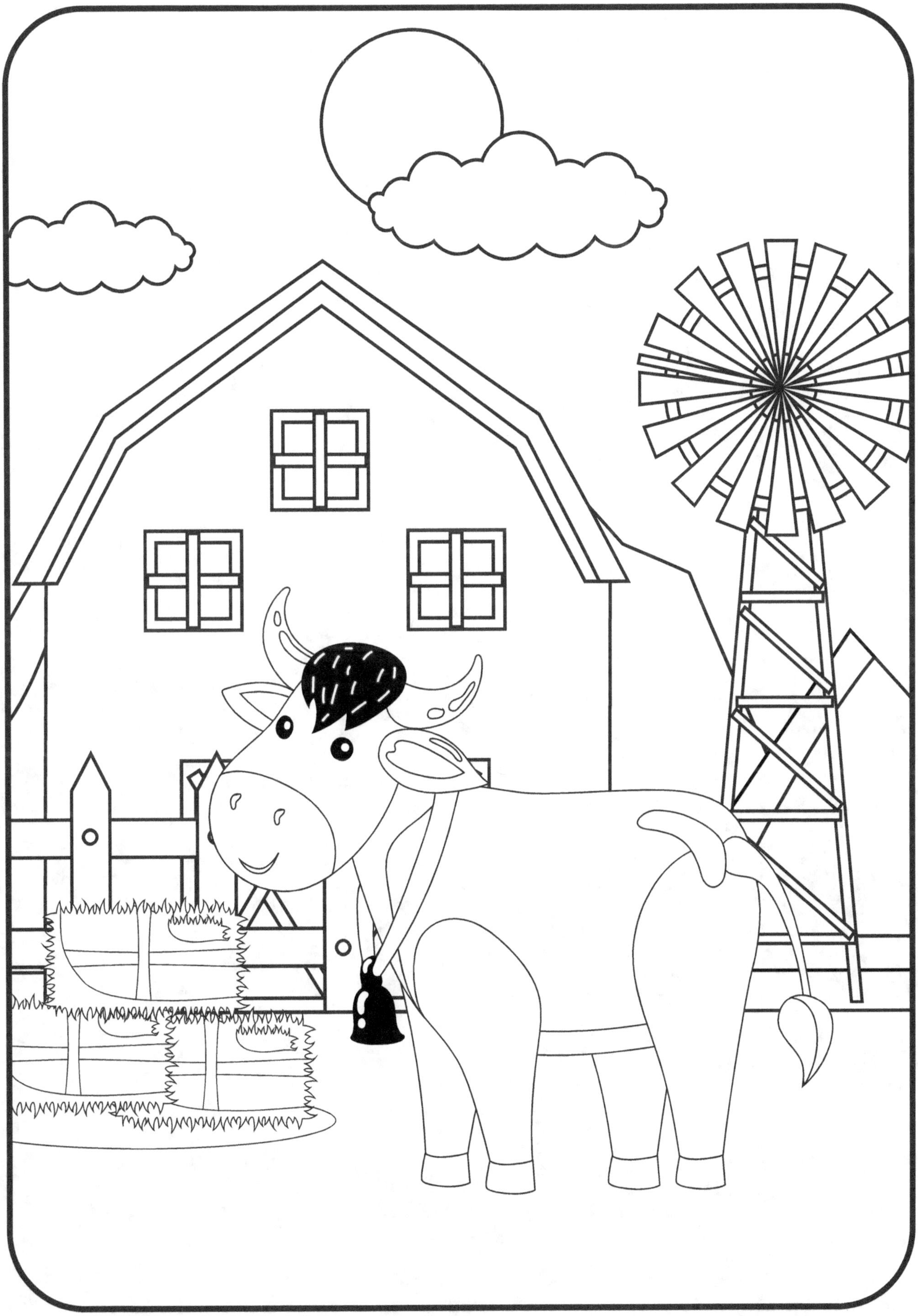

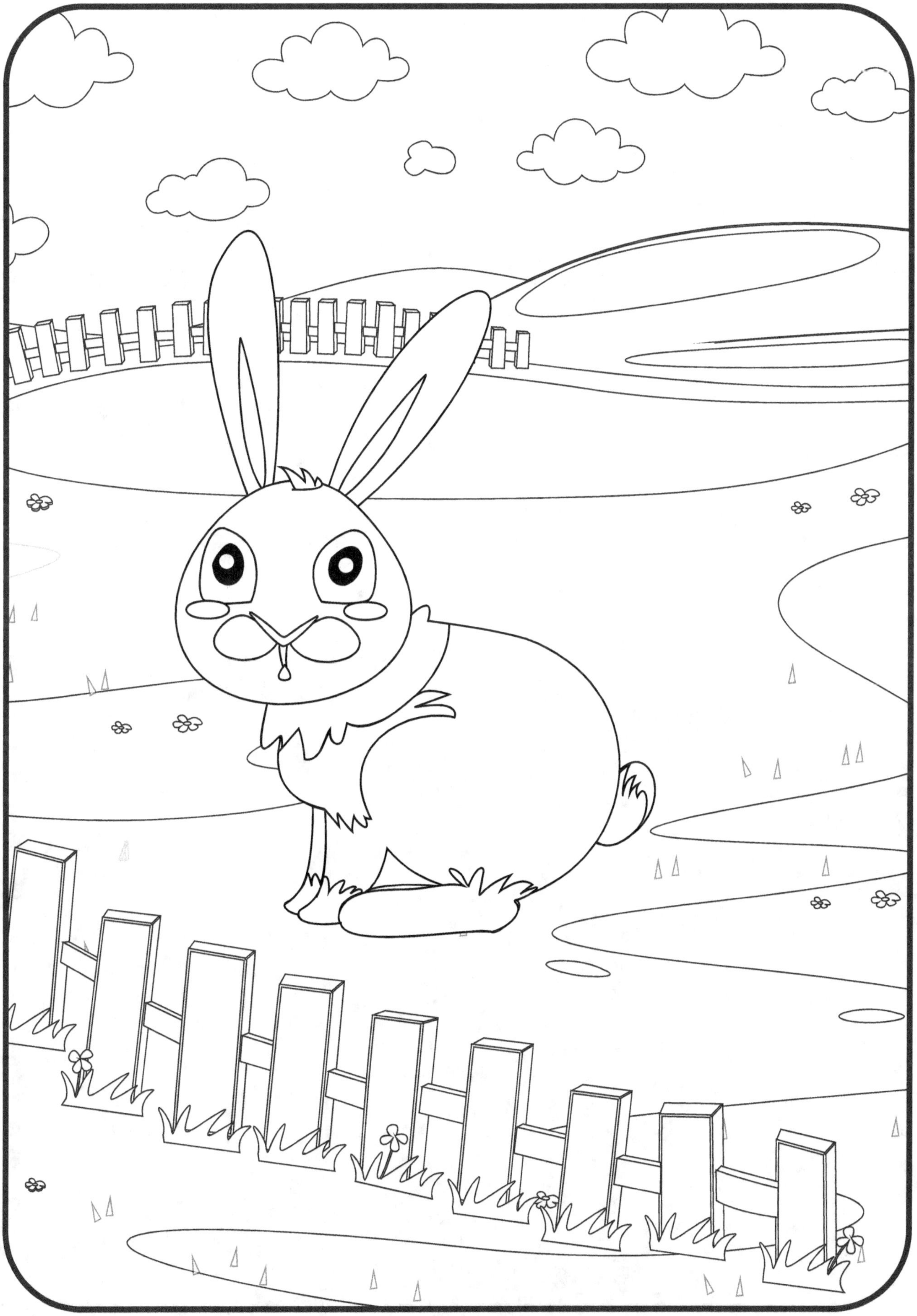

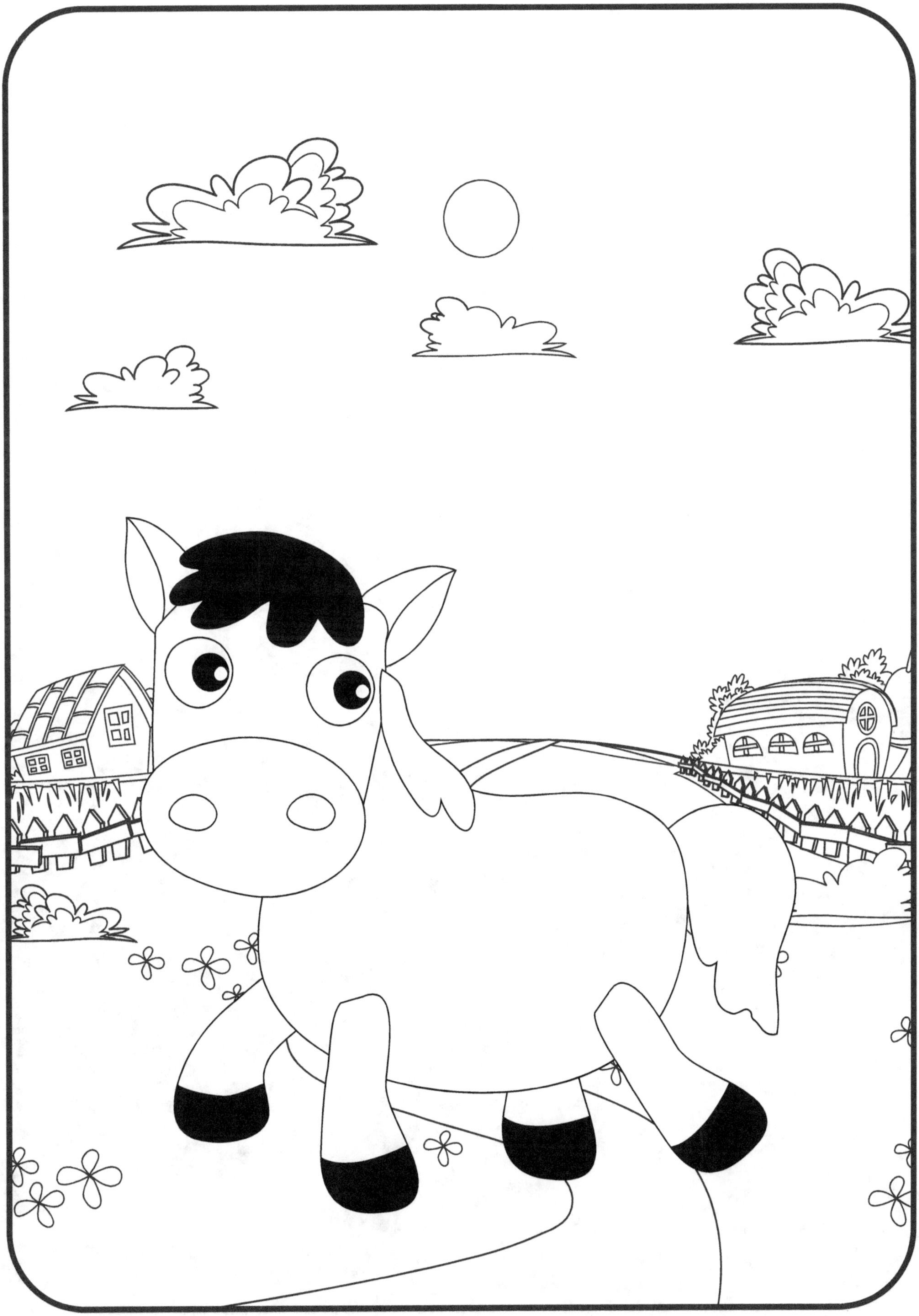

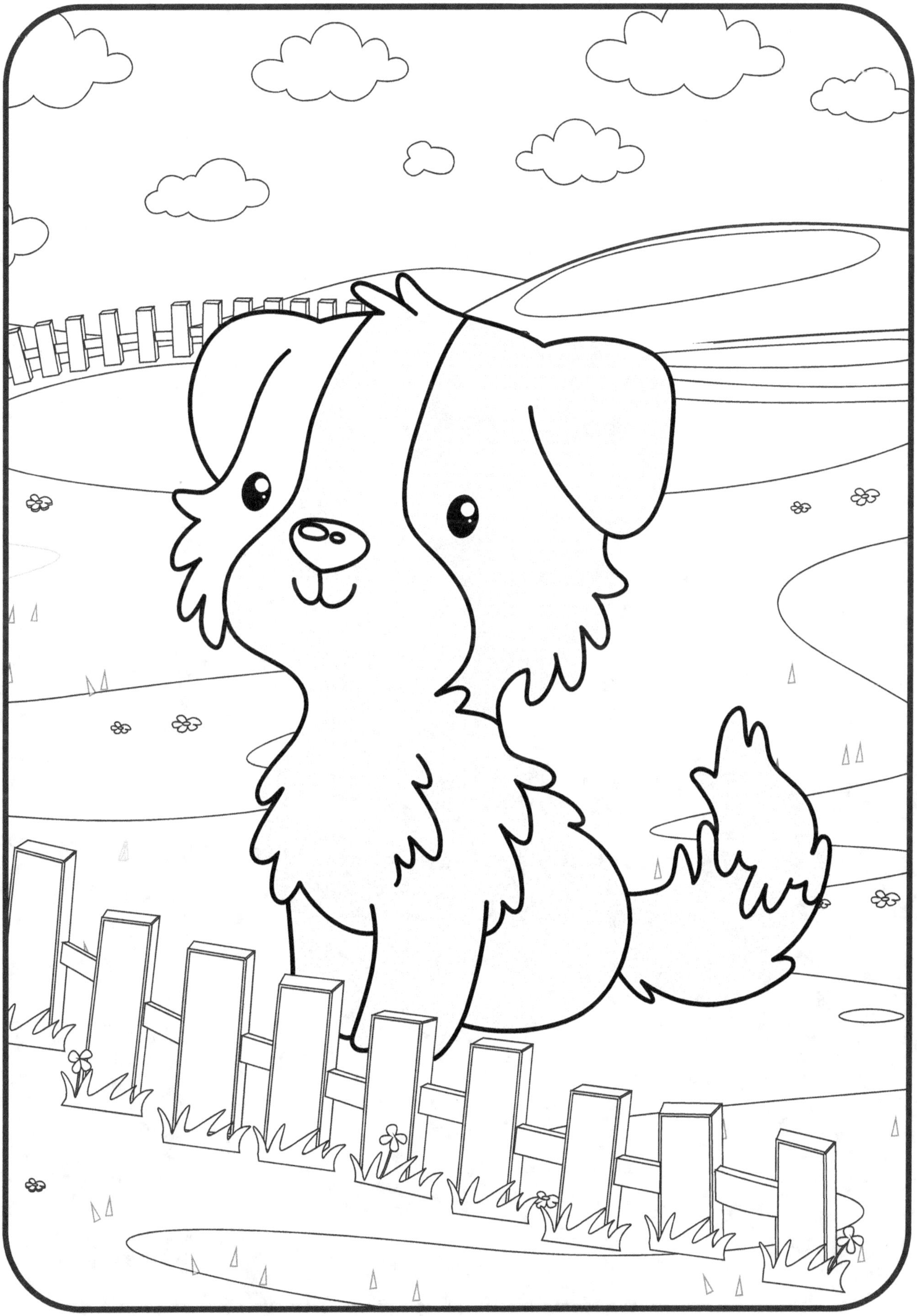

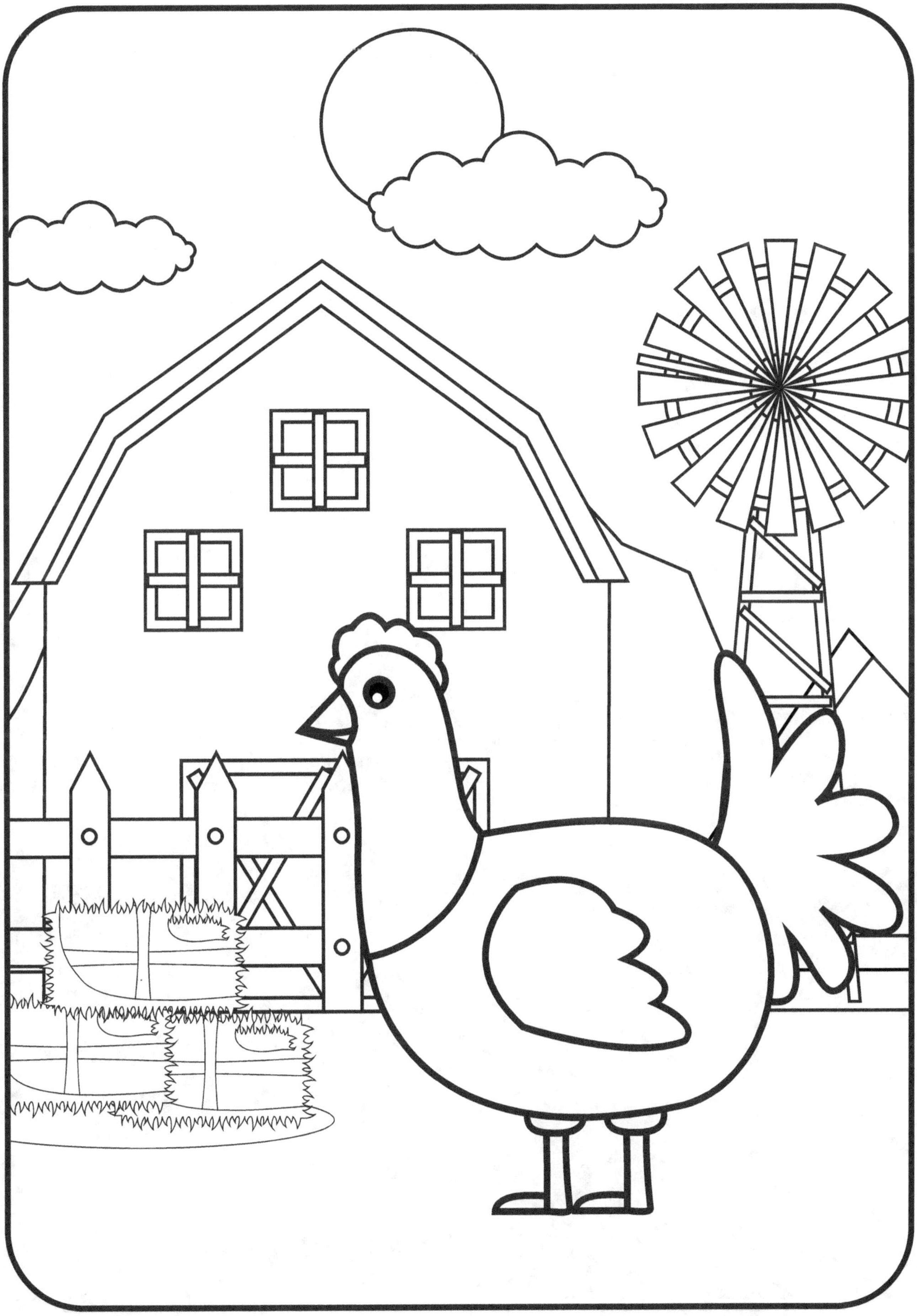

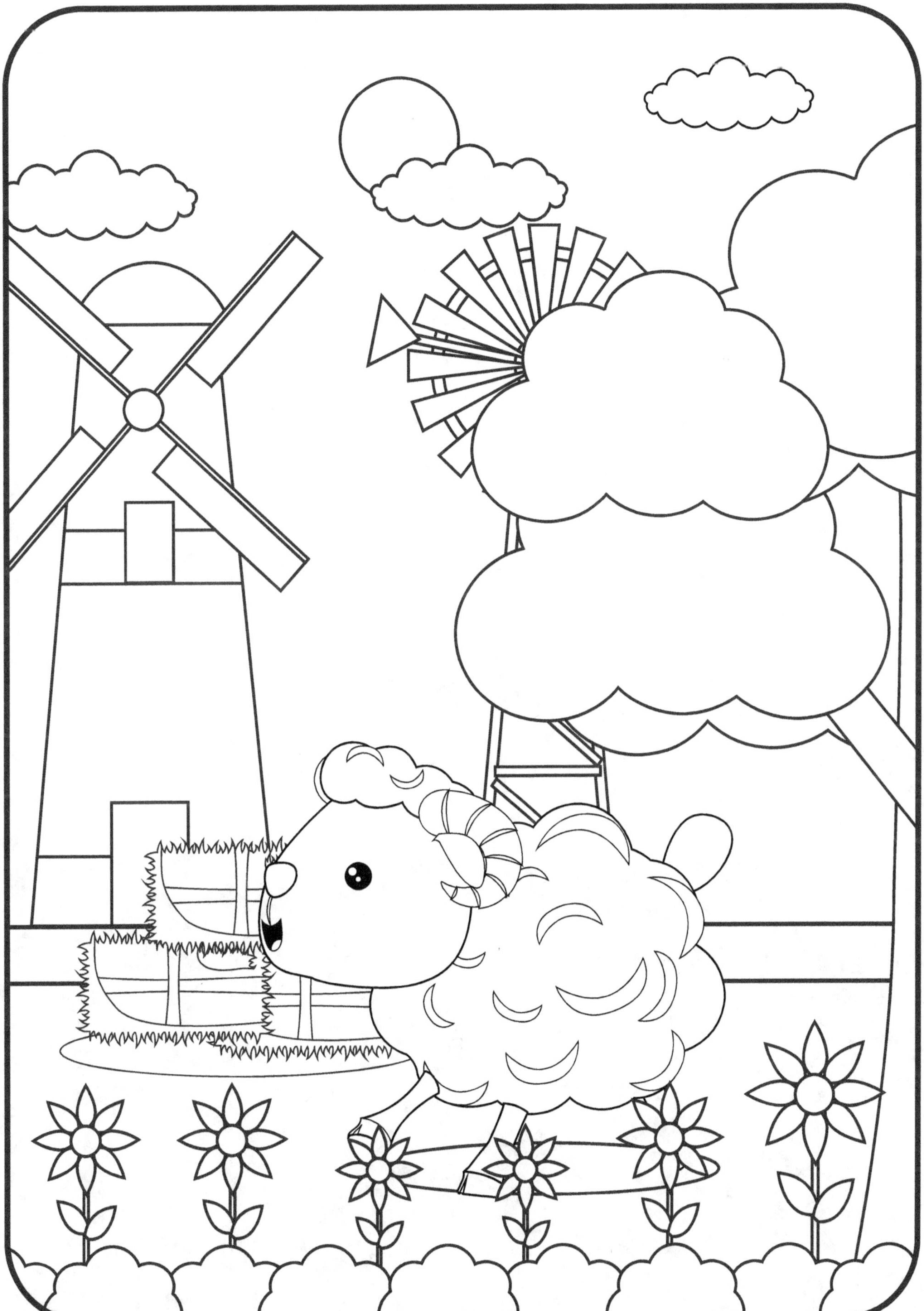

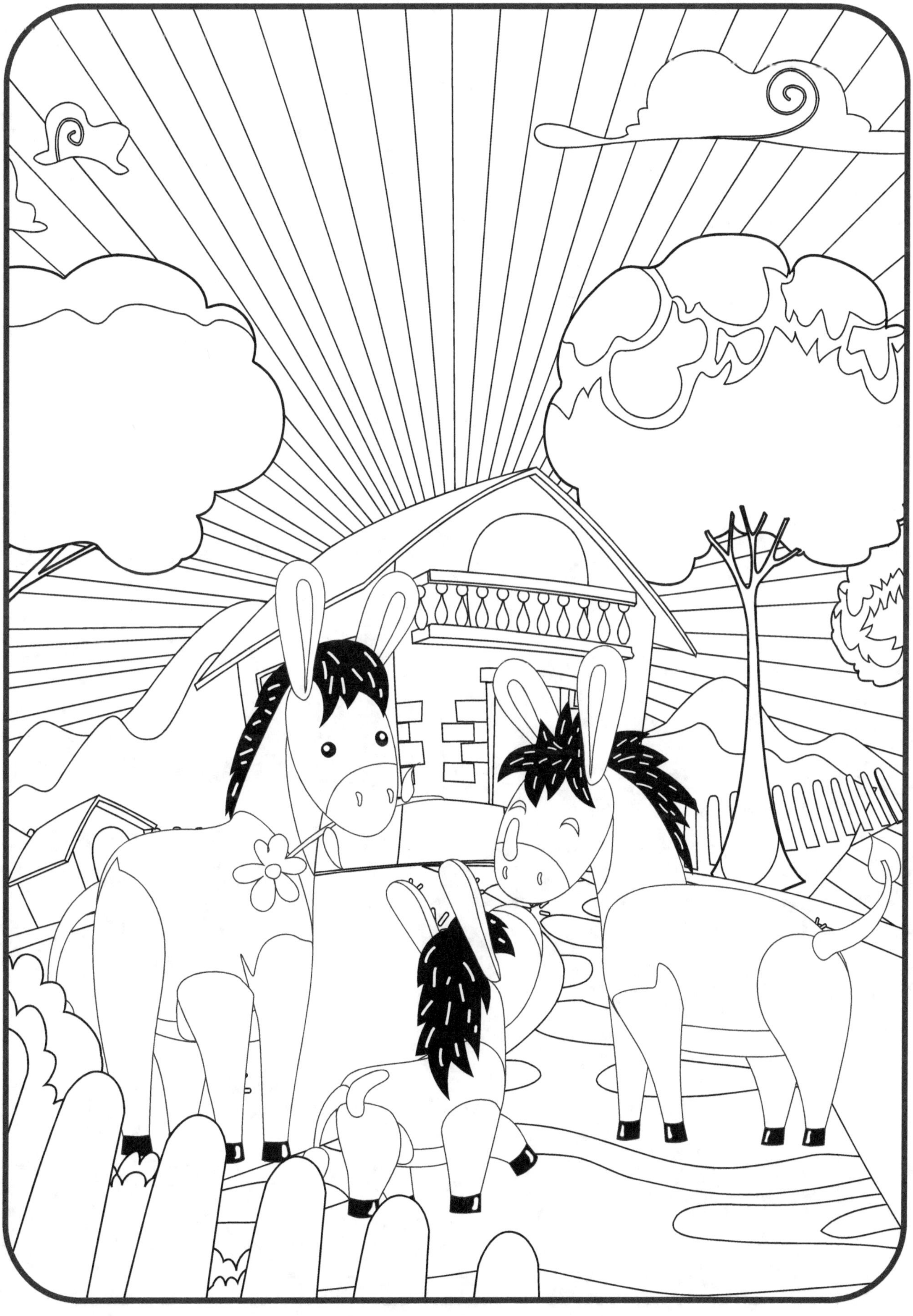

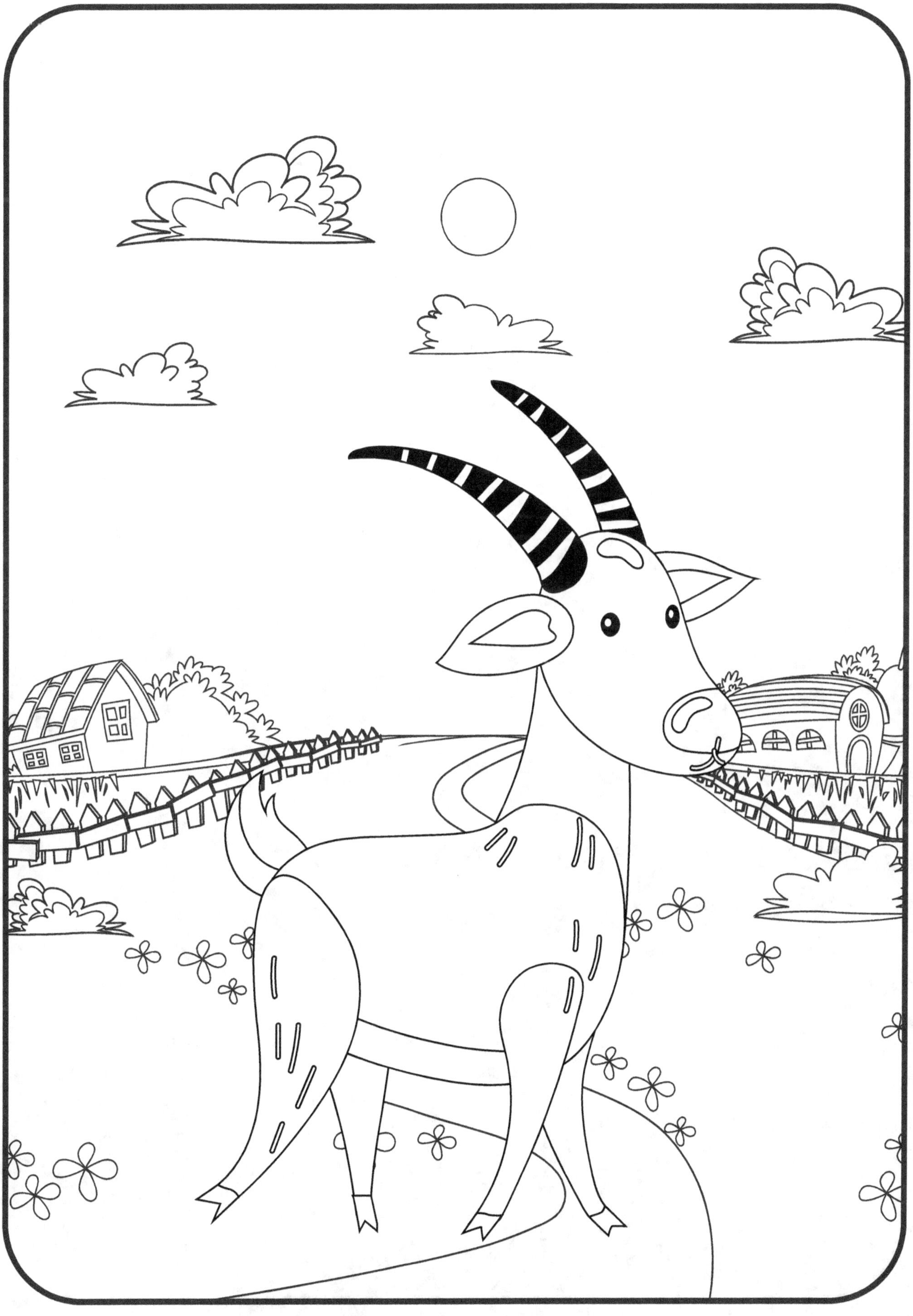

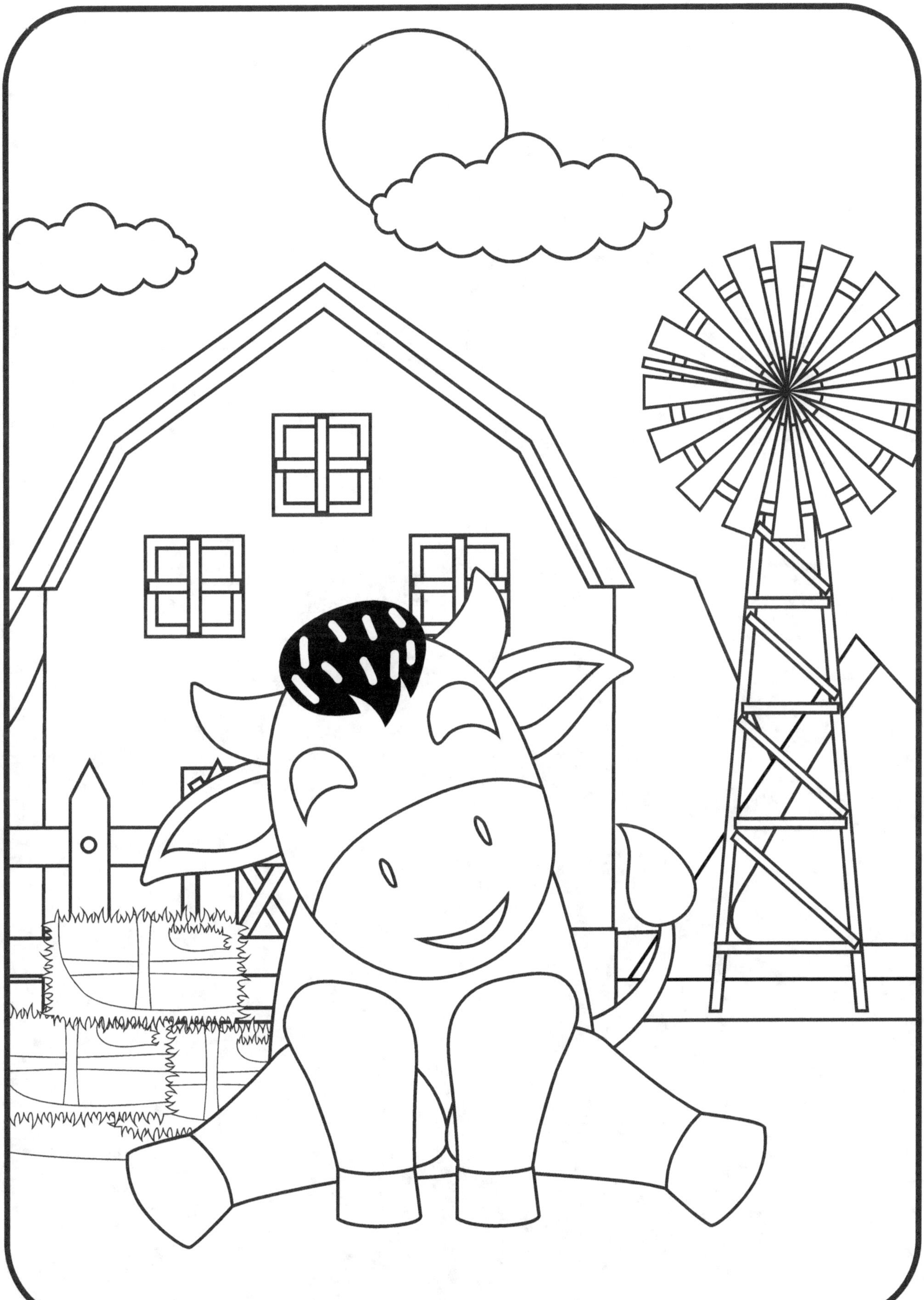

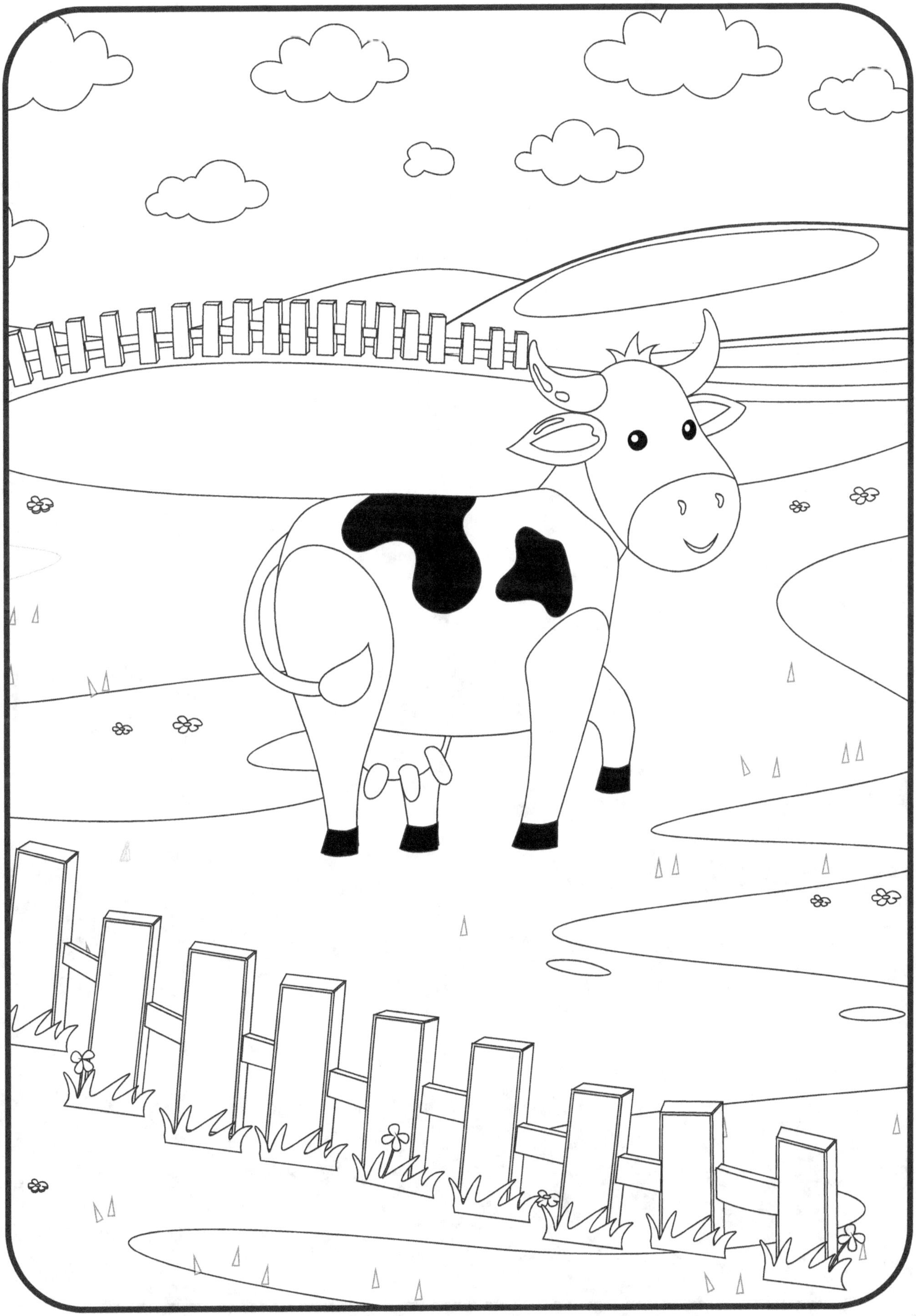

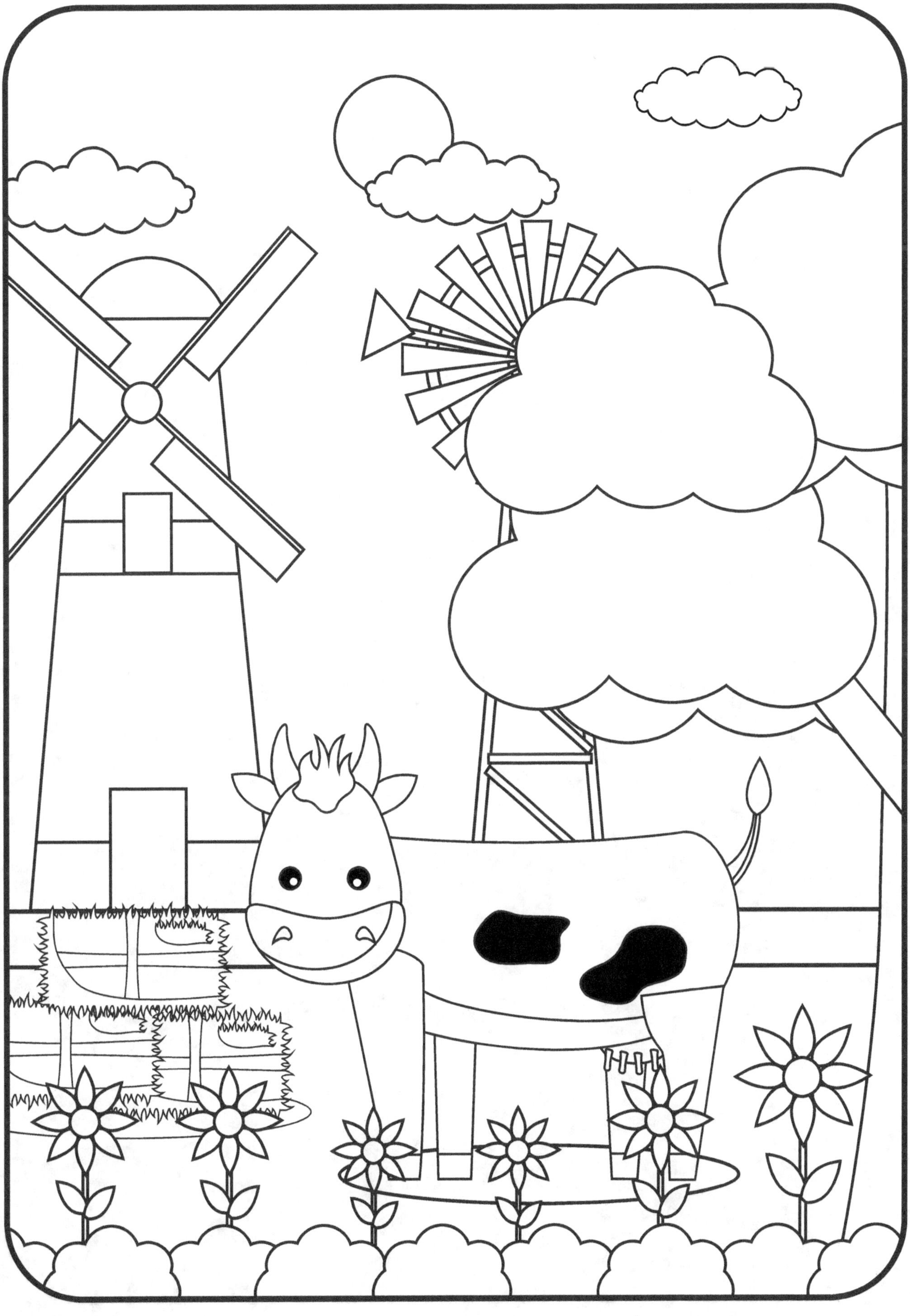

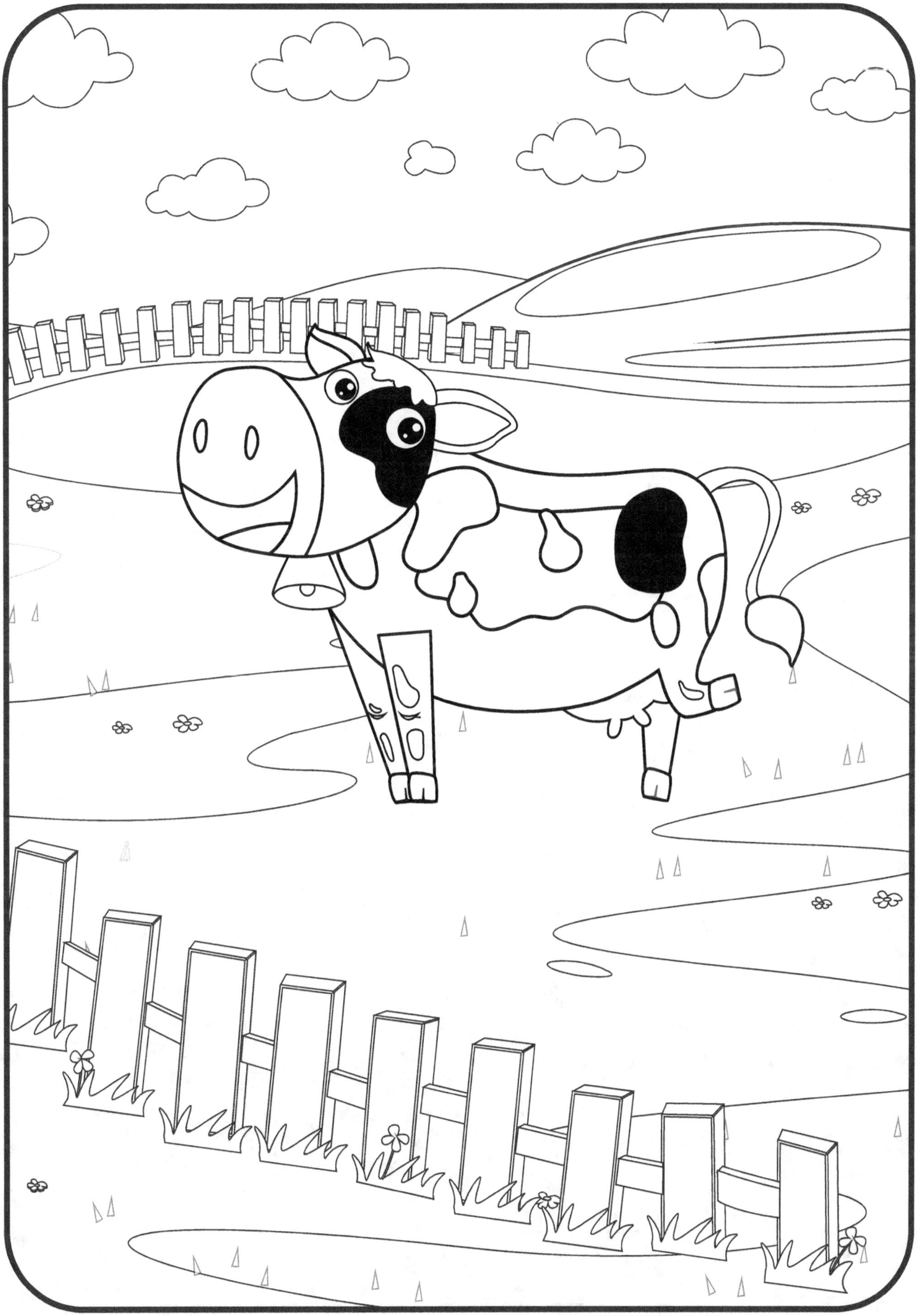

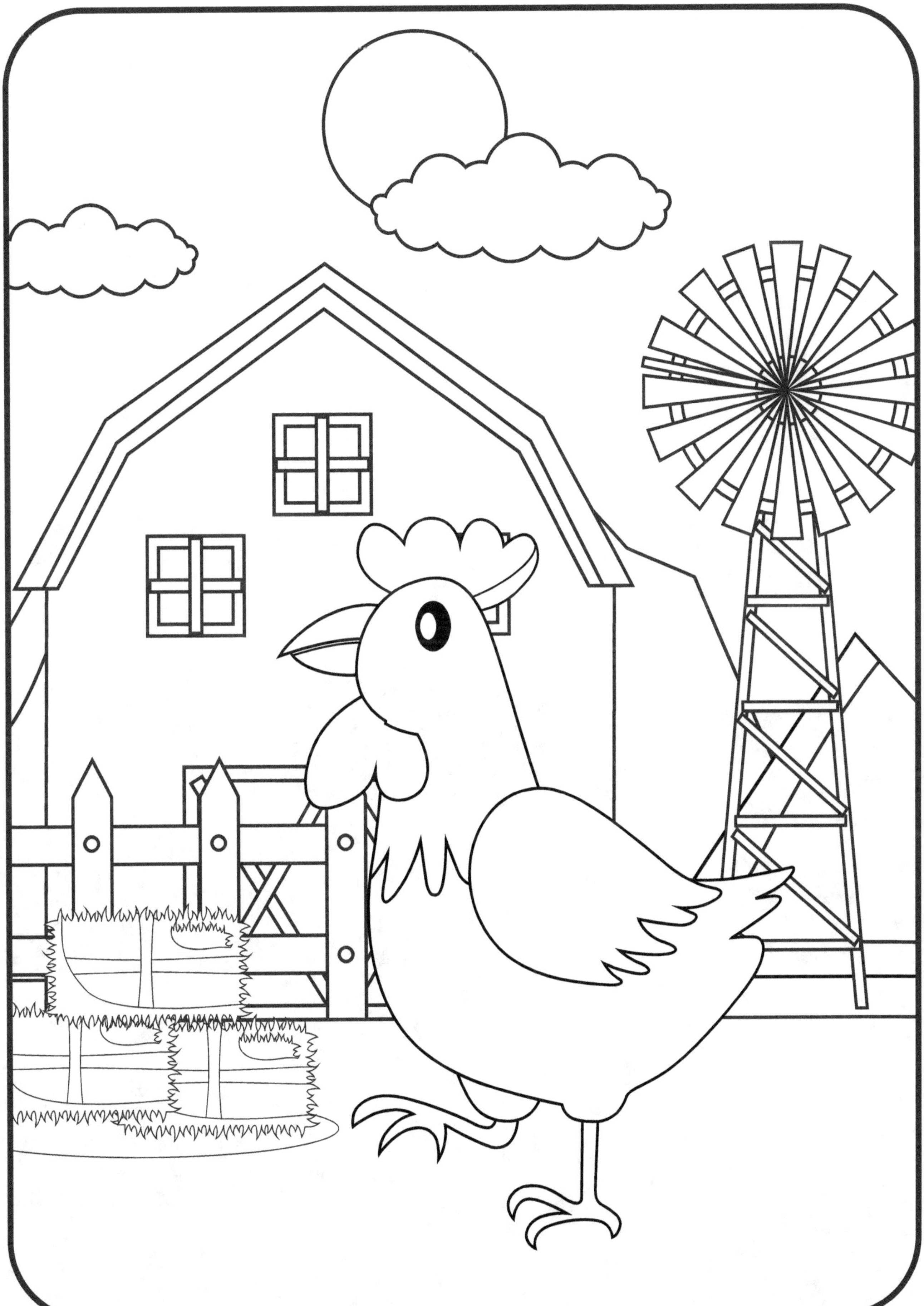

www.ingramcontent.com/pod-product-compliance
Lightning Source LLC
Chambersburg PA
CBHW081538220526
45467CB00010B/3242
9798392816507